COOL

TESSELLATIONS

CREATIVE ACTIVITIES THAT MAKE MATH & SCIENCE
FUN FOR KIDS!

ANDERS HANSON AND ELISSA MANN

A Division of ABDO
ABDO
Publishing Company

VISIT US AT WWW.ABDOPUBLISHING.COM

Published by ABDO Publishing Company, a division of ABDO, P.O. Box 398166, Minneapolis, Minnesota 55439. Copyright ® 2014 by Abdo Consulting Group, Inc. International copyrights reserved in all countries. No part of this book may be reproduced in any form without written permission from the publisher. Checkerboard Library™ is a trademark and logo of ABDO Publishing Company.

Printed in the United States of America, North Mankato, Minnesota
062013
112013

 PRINTED ON RECYCLED PAPER

Design and Production: Anders Hanson, Mighty Media, Inc.
Series Editor: Liz Salzmann
Photo Credits: Anders Hanson Shutterstock, [page 18] MC Escher (image © M.C. Escher Foundation)

LIBRARY OF CONGRESS CATALOGING-IN-PUBLICATION DATA

Hanson, Anders, 1980-
Cool tessellations : creative activities that make math & science fun for kids! / Anders Hanson and Elissa Mann.
    pages cm. -- (Cool art with math & science)
Includes index.
ISBN 978-1-61783-826-2
1. Tessellations (Mathematics)--Juvenile literature. 2. Mathematical recreations--Juvenile literature.
3. Creative activities and seat work--Juvenile literature. I. Mann, Elissa, 1990- II. Title.
QA166.8.H36 2013
516'.132--dc23
                        2013001903

CONTENTS

4 COOL TESSELLATIONS
THE TILING OF SPACE

6 SHAPE UP!
GET TO KNOW YOUR POLYGONS!

8 PROJECT 1
MAKING A TESSELLATION

11 THREE OF A KIND
REGULAR TESSELLATIONS

12 THE GREAT EIGHT
SEMI-REGULAR TESSELLATIONS

13 ANYTHING GOES!
NON-REGULAR TESSELLATIONS

14 PROJECT 2
TESSELLATING WITH SCISSORS

18 M.C. ESCHER
THE MASTER OF TESSELLATIONS

19 MIRROR IMAGE
THE BEAUTY OF SYMMETRY

20 PROJECT 3
TESSELLATING WITH TRACING PAPER

24 ARCHIMEDEAN SOLIDS
TESSELLATIONS ON A SPHERE

26 PROJECT 4
TESSELLATING IN 3-D

30 MATH TERMS

31 GLOSSARY

31 WEB SITES

32 INDEX

COOL

TESSELLATIONS

THE TILING OF SPACE

Take a look at a bee's **honeycomb**. It has **interlocking** shapes that seem to go on forever! A honeycomb is one example of a tessellation. Tessellations are designs with repeating patterns. They don't just occur in nature. People make them too! Tessellations are a way to fill spaces with simple or **complex** shapes.

Bees are good at making a certain kind of tessellation. It's called a **honeycomb**. Each shape has six sides.

For centuries, artists have created patterns with shapes. Can you name any of the shapes in the tessellation below?

SHAPE UP!
GET TO KNOW YOUR POLYGONS!

A polygon is a flat shape. Its sides are straight lines. The sides join together at points called vertices. For any polygon, the number of sides and vertices are the same. For example, all pentagons have five sides and five vertices.

When two lines meet at a vertex, they form an angle. Angles are measured in degrees.

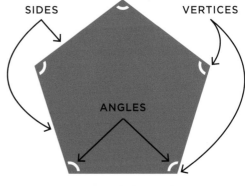

SIDES   VERTICES

ANGLES

A REGULAR PENTAGON

REGULAR POLYGONS

The length of each side is the same.
All of the angles are the same.

EQUILATERAL TRIANGLE   **SQUARE**   **REGULAR PENTAGON**   **REGULAR HEXAGON**

There are two main types of polygons. They are regular and irregular polygons. All of the sides in a regular polygon are the same length. And all of the angles are equal to each other. All other polygons are irregular polygons.

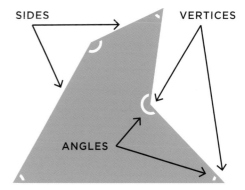

SIDES

VERTICES

ANGLES

AN IRREGULAR PENTAGON

IRREGULAR POLYGONS

If a polygon is not regular, it is an irregular polygon. The sides and angles are not all equal.

TRIANGLE

QUADRILATERAL

PENTAGON

HEXAGON

PROJECT

1 MAKING A TESSELLATION

STUFF YOU'LL NEED

- PENCIL
- RULER
- SCISSORS
- CARD STOCK
- COLORED PAPER

TERMS

- POLYGON
- EQUILATERAL TRIANGLE
- SQUARE
- HEXAGON

There are endless designs you can use in tessellations. A tessellation can be simple, using only a few polygons. Or they can be **complex**, using many different shapes. Start off simple. Make a regular tessellation.

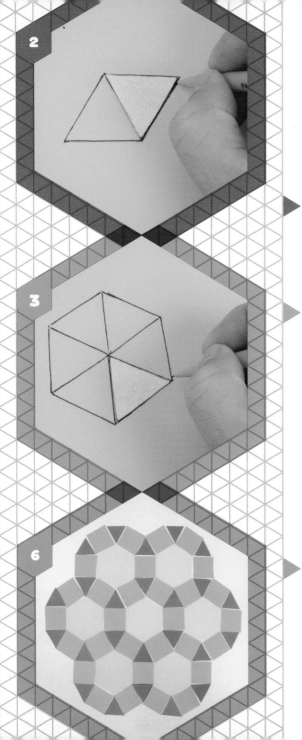

HOW TO MAKE IT

1. Draw an equilateral triangle on card stock. Each side should be 1½ inches (3.8 cm) long. Cut out the triangle. You will use it as a **template**.

2. Trace the template on card stock. Then match the left edge of the template with the right edge of the traced triangle. Trace the template again.

3. Repeat step 2 four more times. The triangles will form a hexagon. Cut out the hexagon. It is another template.

4. Draw a square on card stock. Each side should be 1½ inches (3.8 cm) long. Cut out the square. Now you have three templates.

5. Trace each template ten or more times on colored paper. Cut them out.

6. Use the shapes to create tessellations. Arrange them in different patterns. Fit them together with no **overlapping** or gaps.

THREE OF A KIND
REGULAR TESSELLATIONS

Some tessellations are made with only one polygon. They are called regular tessellations. Only three regular polygons can make regular tessellations. They are the triangle, the square, and the hexagon.

REGULAR TESSELLATIONS

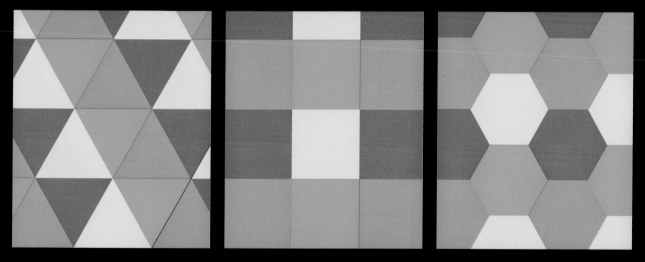

| TRIANGLES | SQUARES | HEXAGONS |

THE GREAT EIGHT
SEMI-REGULAR TESSELLATIONS

A semi-regular tessellation is made with two or more regular polygons. There are eight kinds of semi-regular tessellations.

SEMI-REGULAR TESSELLATIONS

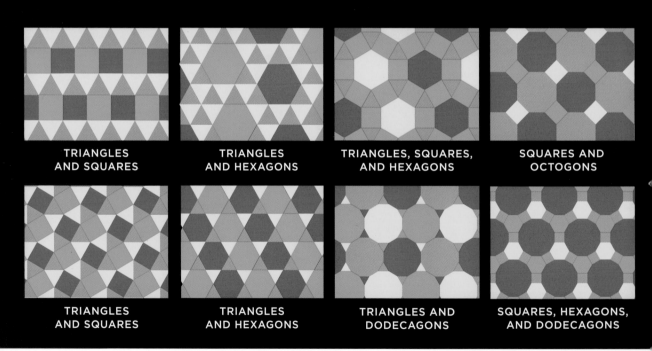

TRIANGLES
AND SQUARES

TRIANGLES
AND HEXAGONS

TRIANGLES, SQUARES,
AND HEXAGONS

SQUARES AND
OCTOGONS

TRIANGLES
AND SQUARES

TRIANGLES
AND HEXAGONS

TRIANGLES AND
DODECAGONS

SQUARES, HEXAGONS,
AND DODECAGONS

ANYTHING GOES!
NON-REGULAR TESSELLATIONS

A non-regular tessellation can be made with many shapes. Any shape can be used, as long as the pattern repeats. Most artistic tessellations are non-regular.

NON-REGULAR TESSELLATIONS

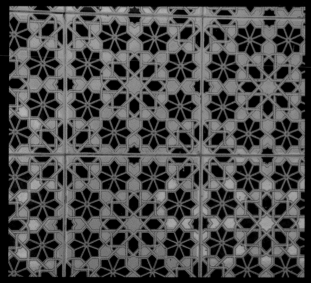

SQUARE MOORISH TILES WITH PRINTED PATTERN

INTERLOCKING MOORISH TILES

PROJECT

2 TESSELLATING WITH SCISSORS

◆◆◆◆◆◆◆◆

STUFF YOU'LL NEED

- CARD STOCK
- RULER
- PENCIL
- SCISSORS
- CLEAR TAPE
- SHEET OF WHITE PAPER
- COLORED PENCILS

TERMS

- RIGHT ANGLE
- VERTICAL
- HORIZONTAL
- SQUARE

There are many different ways to make a tessellation. Try creating a non-regular tessellation. When it is finished, you will have a **unique** poster to hang up.

20240544

HOW TO MAKE IT

1   Use a ruler and pencil to draw a 2-inch (5 cm) square on card stock. Cut it out.

2   Label each corner of the square with the numbers 1 through 4. Draw a horizontal **squiggly** line from edge to edge. Draw a vertical squiggly line from edge to edge. No line should go through a corner of the square.

3   Cut the sections apart along the squiggly lines. Each section should have a corner of the square. The corners are right angles.

4   Rearrange the sections. The four corners should meet in the center. Tape them together to form a **template**.

5   Trace the **template** on a
sheet of white paper.

6   Rotate the template so one edge
matches the shape you traced. Trace
the template again. Repeat until
the paper is covered. There should
be no gaps between the shapes.

7   Color the tessellation. Hang your
tessellation poster on a wall.

M.C. ESCHER
THE MASTER OF TESSELLATIONS

M.C. Escher was an artist famous for his tessellations. He used geometric shapes and symmetry to create much of his art.

Escher was influenced by geometric tiling he saw in Moorish palaces. For examples of Moorish tiles see page 13.

MIRROR IMAGE
THE BEAUTY OF SYMMETRY

Symmetry is an important part of making tessellations. Shapes repeated in a pattern create symmetry. There are many different types of symmetry. Three types of symmetry often found in tessellations are translational, rotational, and reflectional.

PATTERN SYMMETRY

Translational
The shape slides up, down, to the sides, or diagonally while keeping its form.

Rotational
The shape turns in a circular direction to the right or to the left while keeping its form.

Reflectional
The shape mirrors itself onto a different part of the tessellation.

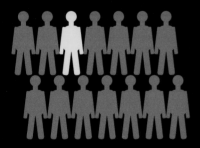

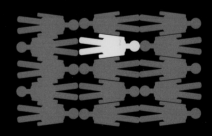

PROJECT 3

TESSELLATING WITH TRACING PAPER

STUFF YOU'LL NEED

- 2 SHEETS OF WHITE PAPER
- RULER
- PENCIL
- 2 SHEETS OF TRACING PAPER
- COLORED MARKERS

TERMS

- TRANSLATIONAL SYMMETRY
- SQUARE

Use translational symmetry to make a new kind of tessellation! Use your **imagination** to create new shapes. The weirdest shapes can make the coolest projects!

HOW TO MAKE IT

1 Use a pencil and a ruler to draw a 2-inch (5 cm) square on white paper. Draw a **squiggly** line over the top edge of the square. Draw a squiggly line over the right edge of the square.

2 Erase the straight lines **underneath** the squiggly lines.

3 Put tracing paper over the shape. Trace the two squiggly lines. Slide the tracing paper to the right. Match the empty left edge to the right squiggly line on the white paper. Trace the line.

4   Line up the two side **squiggly** lines
    with either end of the top line on the
    white paper. Trace the top line.

5   Lay a second sheet of tracing paper
    over the first sheet. Trace the
    shape. Remove the white paper.

6   Slide the second sheet to the right. The
    left side of the shape on the second
    sheet will match the right side of the
    shape on the first sheet. Trace the
    shape. Slide the second sheet down.
    Match the top of the shape on the
    second sheet to the bottom of the shape
    on the first sheet. Trace the shape.

7   Repeat step 6 until the page is full. Color
    in the shapes. Hang it in a window
    for a **stained glass** tessellation.

ARCHIMEDEAN SOLIDS
TESSELLATIONS ON A SPHERE

Archimedean solids are three-dimensional shapes. The surface of an Archimedean solid is a tessellation. Two or more types of regular polygons make up the surface. A truncated tetrahedron is one example. It has four triangles and four hexagons.

TRUNCATED TETRAHEDRON

4 triangles
4 hexagons

CUBOCTAHEDRON

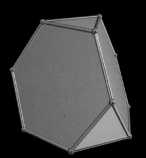

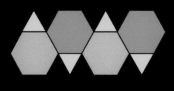

There are 13 Archimedean solids. The three shown below are special. They will fit together with no gaps between them. That's tessellating in three dimensions!

8 triangles
6 squares

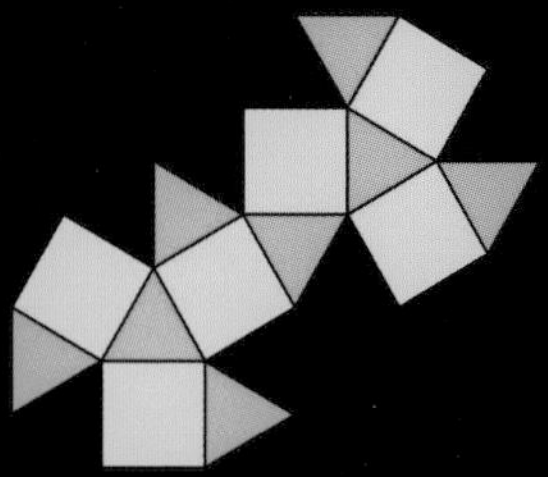

TRUNCATED OCTAHEDRON

6 squares
8 hexagons

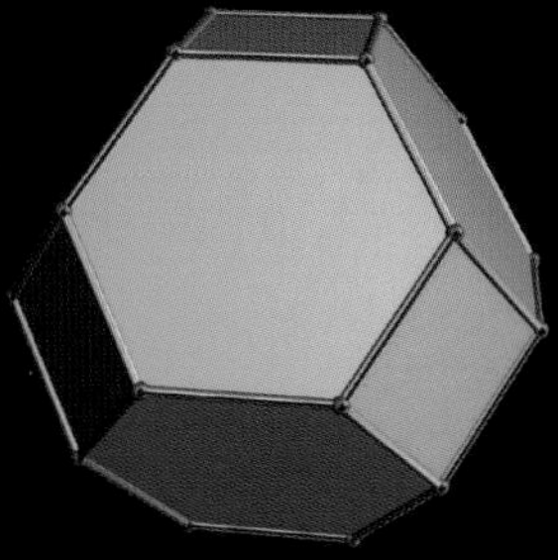

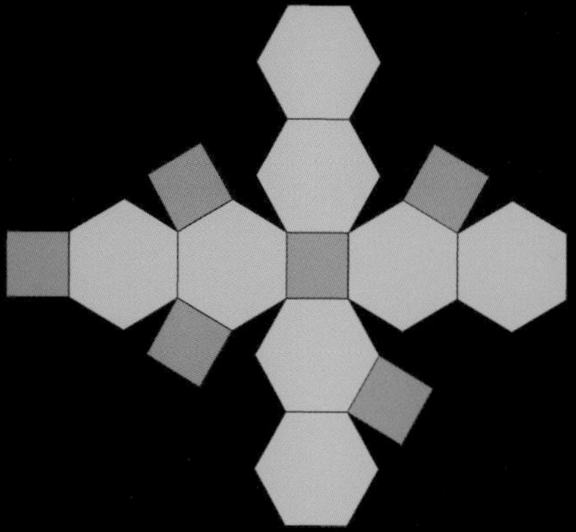

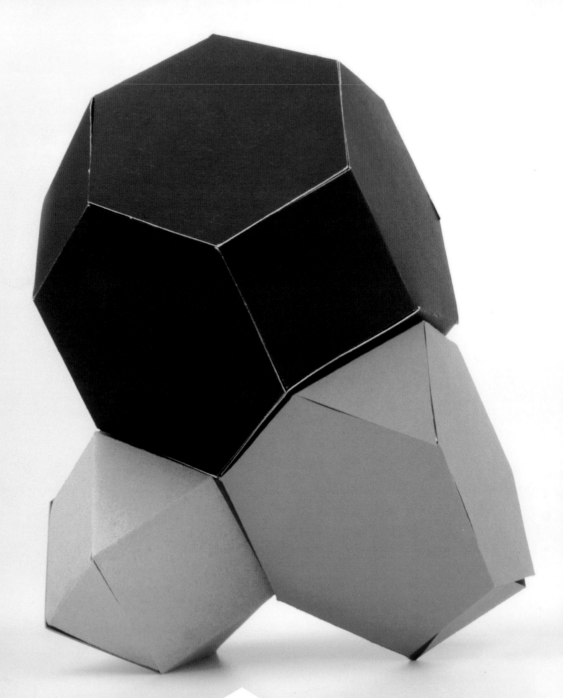

PROJECT 4

TESSELLATING IN 3-D

You have been making tessellations on paper. For the final project, you will make a 3-D tessellation! First, make the Archimedean solids. Then fit them together so they fill space. It's a geometric puzzle in 3-D!

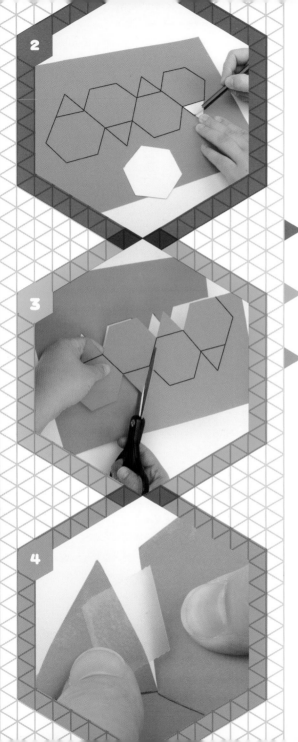

MAKE THE SOLIDS

1   Arrange the paper shape
    templates from Project 1 (page
    10) on card stock. Copy the
    layout on page 24 to create the
    truncated tetrahedron pattern.

2   Trace the pattern. Trace all the
    way around each shape.

3   Cut out the pattern. Fold on
    the remaining lines. Unfold.

4   See the tips for taping the polygon
    edges on page 29. Place tape along an
    edge. Some tape should hang over.
    Tape it to the nearest open side edge
    to the right. Tape all the polygons
    with the least number of sides first.
    Then tape the larger polygons.

5   Put the shape templates in the
    cuboctahedron layout (see page
    25). Repeat steps 2 through 4.

6   Put the shape templates in the
    truncated octahedron layout (see
    page 25). Repeat steps 2 through 4.

FIT THE SOLIDS TOGETHER

1 Find faces on two of the solids that are the same shape. Match them together. Balance them on top of each other.

2 Fit the third solid between the first two solids. The third solid will match one face to each of the first two solids.

3 Make more solids to add. You will need a truncated tetrahedron for every cuboctahedron and truncated octahedron you make. Add one new solid to the structure at a time. Match at least two faces of the solid in the structure.

TIPS FOR TAPING POLYGON EDGES

» If 5 or 3 sides of a polygon are open, tape the two rightmost sides.

» If 2 sides of a polygon are open, tape the rightmost side.

» If 1 side of a polygon is open, tape it.

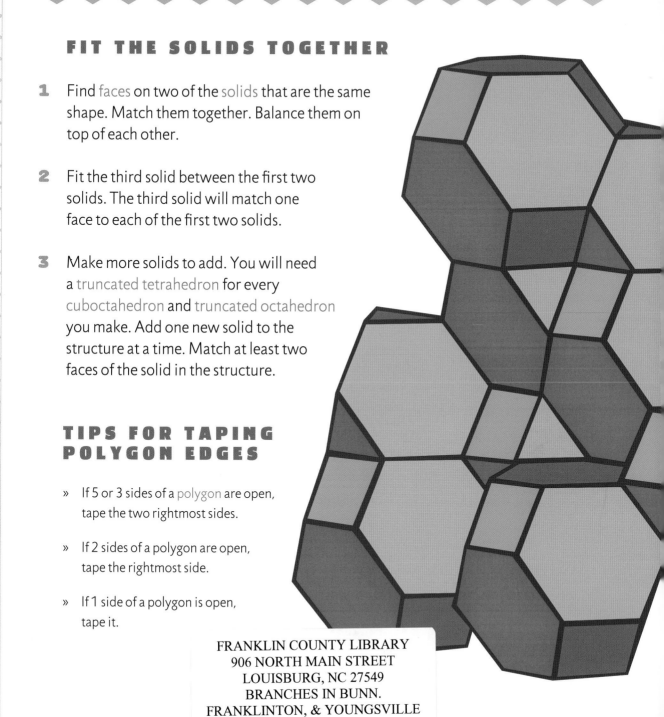

MATH TERMS

CUBOCTAHEDRON - a 3-D shape with eight triangular faces and six square faces.

EQUILATERAL TRIANGLE - a triangle with sides that are all the same length.

FACE - a polygon that forms one of the flat surfaces of a 3-D shape.

GEOMETRIC - made up of straight lines, circles, and other shapes.

HEXAGON - a shape with six straight sides and six angles.

HORIZONTAL - in the same direction as the ground, or side-to-side.

POLYGON - a two-dimensional shape with any number of sides and angles.

RIGHT ANGLE - an angle that measures 90 degrees.

SOLID - a shape that takes up space in three dimensions. Also called a 3-D shape.

SQUARE - a shape with four straight, equal sides and four equal angles.

TRANSLATIONAL SYMMETRY - a pattern with one or more elements that repeat to either side or up or down.

TRUNCATED OCTAHEDRON - a 3-D shape with eight hexagonal faces and six square faces.

TRUNCATED TETRAHEDRON - a 3-D shape with four hexagonal faces and four triangular faces.

VERTICAL - in the opposite direction from the ground, or up-and-down.

GLOSSARY

COMPLEX - made of many parts.

HONEYCOMB - a structure that bees make out of wax.

IMAGINATION - the creative ability to think up new ideas and form mental images of things that aren't real or present.

INTERLOCKING - having parts that fit together and connect tightly.

OVERLAP - to lie partly on top of something.

SQUIGGLY - wavy or curvy.

STAINED GLASS - colored glass used to make a picture or design in a window.

TEMPLATE - a shape you draw or cut around to copy it onto something else.

UNDERNEATH - under or below something else.

UNIQUE - different, unusual, or special.

WEB SITES

To learn more about math and science, visit ABDO Publishing Company on the World Wide Web at www.abdopublishing.com. Web sites about creative ways for kids to experience math and science are featured on our Book Links page. These links are routinely monitored and updated to provide the most current information available.

INDEX

A

Archimedean solids
definition of, 24
project for, 27–29
qualities of, 24–25
types of, 24–25
Artistic
tessellations,
5, 13, 18

E

Escher, M. C., 18

H

Hexagons, 6, 7, 11
Honeycombs, 4, 5

I

Irregular
polygons, 7

M

Moorish palaces
and tiles, 13, 18

N

Non-regular
tessellations
project for, 15–17
qualities of, 13

P

Polygons
definition of, 6
qualities of, 6
types of, 6, 7, 11

R

Reflectional
symmetry, 19
Regular polygons,
6, 7, 11, 24

Regular
tessellations
project for, 9–10
qualities of, 11
Rotational
symmetry, 19

S

Semi-regular
tessellations, 12
Squares, 6, 11
Symmetry, 19

T

Templates, 10, 16–17
Tessellations
definition of, 4
projects for,
9–10, 15–17,
21–23, 27–29
qualities of,
4–5, 11, 19

types of, 4, 5,
9, 11–13, 24–25
Three-dimensional
shapes
project for, 27–29
qualities of, 24
types of, 24–25
Translational
symmetry
definition of, 19
project using,
21–23
Triangles, 6, 7, 11

W

Web sites, about
math and
science, 31